A poem, on the Parliament. By George Waldron, ...

George Waldron

ECCO
PRINT EDITIONS

A poem, on the Parliament. By George Waldron, ...
Waldron, George
ESTCID: N011773
Reproduction from Huntington Library
With a half-title.
London : printed in the year, 1718.
[4],12p. ; 8°

ECCO

Eighteenth Century Collections Online Print Editions

Gale ECCO Print Editions

Relive history with *Eighteenth Century Collections Online*, now available in print for the independent historian and collector. This series includes the most significant English-language and foreign-language works printed in Great Britain during the eighteenth century, and is organized in seven different subject areas including literature and language; medicine, science, and technology; and religion and philosophy. The collection also includes thousands of important works from the Americas.

The eighteenth century has been called "The Age of Enlightenment." It was a period of rapid advance in print culture and publishing, in world exploration, and in the rapid growth of science and technology – all of which had a profound impact on the political and cultural landscape. At the end of the century the American Revolution, French Revolution and Industrial Revolution, perhaps three of the most significant events in modern history, set in motion developments that eventually dominated world political, economic, and social life.

In a groundbreaking effort, Gale initiated a revolution of its own: digitization of epic proportions to preserve these invaluable works in the largest online archive of its kind. Contributions from major world libraries constitute over 175,000 original printed works. Scanned images of the actual pages, rather than transcriptions, recreate the works ***as they first appeared.***

Now for the first time, these high-quality digital scans of original works are available via print-on-demand, making them readily accessible to libraries, students, independent scholars, and readers of all ages.

For our initial release we have created seven robust collections to form one the world's most comprehensive catalogs of 18th century works.

Initial Gale ECCO Print Editions collections include:

> ***History and Geography***
> Rich in titles on English life and social history, this collection spans the world as it was known to eighteenth-century historians and explorers. Titles include a wealth of travel accounts and diaries, histories of nations from throughout the world, and maps and charts of a world that was still being discovered. Students of the War of American Independence will find fascinating accounts from the British side of conflict.

Social Science

Delve into what it was like to live during the eighteenth century by reading the first-hand accounts of everyday people, including city dwellers and farmers, businessmen and bankers, artisans and merchants, artists and their patrons, politicians and their constituents. Original texts make the American, French, and Industrial revolutions vividly contemporary.

Medicine, Science and Technology

Medical theory and practice of the 1700s developed rapidly, as is evidenced by the extensive collection, which includes descriptions of diseases, their conditions, and treatments. Books on science and technology, agriculture, military technology, natural philosophy, even cookbooks, are all contained here.

Literature and Language

Western literary study flows out of eighteenth-century works by Alexander Pope, Daniel Defoe, Henry Fielding, Frances Burney, Denis Diderot, Johann Gottfried Herder, Johann Wolfgang von Goethe, and others. Experience the birth of the modern novel, or compare the development of language using dictionaries and grammar discourses.

Religion and Philosophy

The Age of Enlightenment profoundly enriched religious and philosophical understanding and continues to influence present-day thinking. Works collected here include masterpieces by David Hume, Immanuel Kant, and Jean-Jacques Rousseau, as well as religious sermons and moral debates on the issues of the day, such as the slave trade. The Age of Reason saw conflict between Protestantism and Catholicism transformed into one between faith and logic -- a debate that continues in the twenty-first century.

Law and Reference

This collection reveals the history of English common law and Empire law in a vastly changing world of British expansion. Dominating the legal field is the *Commentaries of the Law of England* by Sir William Blackstone, which first appeared in 1765. Reference works such as almanacs and catalogues continue to educate us by revealing the day-to-day workings of society.

Fine Arts

The eighteenth-century fascination with Greek and Roman antiquity followed the systematic excavation of the ruins at Pompeii and Herculaneum in southern Italy; and after 1750 a neoclassical style dominated all artistic fields. The titles here trace developments in mostly English-language works on painting, sculpture, architecture, music, theater, and other disciplines. Instructional works on musical instruments, catalogs of art objects, comic operas, and more are also included.

A
POEM,
ON THE
PARLIAMENT.

A
POEM,
ON THE
PARLIAMENT.

By GEORGE WALDRON, late of
Queen's College, *Oxon*.

Dulce est pro Patria-----

LONDON:
Printed in the Year MDCCXVIII.

A

POEM,

ON THE

PARLIAMENT.

WHEN daring *Poets* would *Encomiums* raiſe
Worthy ſuch *Patriots* as adorn our Days,
Pindar's ſublimeſt flights too humble ſeem
To be Embelliſhments for ſuch a Theme;
When *Senates* are the Subjects of our Muſe,
The Tuneful Nine can but due Thoughts infuſe:
Our Antient Bards, who *Britain*'s Glories wrote,
How well She Counſell'd, and how bravely Fought,

Could they review the Acts of later Times,
Would raise their Fancy to more noble Rhimes,
And Mighty EDWRAD's Warlike Deeds must yield,
To ANNA's Conquest at fam'd *Blenhiems* Field:
But since those brave Heroic Souls are laid,
Thoughtless of Us, amongst the silent Dead,
My Muse with equal Zeal, but humbler Lays,
Attempts to blazon Modern *Patriots* praise.

HAIL awful Sirs! Blest Guardians of our Isle!
May Heaven assent and on your Counsels smile;
Europa big with Expectation waits,
For the Result of your August Debates,
Her Ballance rest's in your decisive Hand
Whose mutual Concord gives the World Command:
Tho' fierce BELLONA, proudly storms in *Spain*,
Britannia rides Triumphant on the Main,
And Happy GEORGE revives ELIZA's Reign,
Then WALSINGHAM and CECIL brightly shone,
Unbyass'd Champions for a threatned Crown;
Most Glorious Queen! Her *Senate* Wise, and True,
Unmatch'd in Story, till we write of You.

Most

WHEN hoſtile Bands aſſail'd victorious *Rome*,
She ſought no Succours, but her Friends at home,
Her truſty Counſels prov'd ſucceſsful Charms,
To Guard their State againſt Impending Harms,
'Till the World trembled at her conqu'ring Arms:
Now Foreign Troops Great CÆSAR's Rights invade,
He courts *Britannia* for her friendly Aid,
Britannia ever Famous for Renown,
At once defends her ſelf, and CÆSAR's Crown:
Inſulted Friends abroad with watchful Eye,
Expect your *needful* Unanimity,
(The ſtrongeſt *Bulwark* and the beſt *Allie*,)
The future Welfare of depending States,
Auſpicious *Patriots*! On your Influence waits:
Their Hopes are vain, who would rejoice to ſee
Our Sov'reign, and his *Senate* diſagree.

WHEN treach'rous Faction its Contagion ſpread,
And proud Rebellion rear'd her daring Head,

Then your united Force did bravely quell,
The raging Monſter, and diſſolve the Spell:
As at *Preſtonia*'s Memorable Fight,
Where Loyal Troops urg'd trait'rous Arms to Flight,
So *Britain*'s Foes with conſcious Guilt muſt fall,
Whilſt ſuch true Champions guard her Capitol.

PRIDE of your Sov'reign, and your Country too,
Whoſe Int'reſt is the Object of your View,
Under your Wing *Britannia*'s ſafety lies,
Thoughtleſs of Wrong, fearleſs of Injuries,
A Refuge, more ſecure there cannot be,
Than with the Oracles of Equity;
Shall the *Batavians* boaſt a thriving Trade,
And Wealthy *London*, droop her noble Head?
Shall new born Fears reſtrain her wonted Courſe,
Bleſt with ſo wiſe a Prince, ſo brave a Force?
Not ſo; her floating Barks ſhall ſail at large,
Neptune obey at Sea, at Home Great GEORGE:
Her Injur'd Merchants ſhall Complain no more,
Nor dread freſh Inſults from a Foreign Pow'r,

Our

Our Monarch's Care, and faithful *Senates* skill,
Will make fair *London*, *Europe's* Miſtreſs ſtill.

WHILST Armies are not call'd to foreign Wars,
Nor wanted to ſuppreſs domeſtick Jars,
Whilſt Troops (of late ſo uſeful) are diſcharg'd,
And neither our Expence, nor Fears inlarg'd,
What Loyal *British* Subject will complain,
To ſee our Bulwarks floating on the Main?
That Iſland's ſafety doth the charge reward,
Where naval Forces, are the Nations Guard.
'Twas threatning Danger, that was near in View,
Firſt caus'd ſuch Wiſe Aſſemblies (Sirs) as You,
A prudent Method, for ſo great a Choice,
To ſave the Publick by a publick Voice:
Each Place the Worthieſt of their *Patriots* ſent,
They Proud to chooſe, and He to Repreſent,
The faithful *Senates* zeal Maintain'd their Laws,
The Subjects Freedom grac'd the Glorious Cauſe,
Whilſt Prince, and People ſhar'd the Grand Applauſe.

And

And you Illustrious Guardians at the Helm,
With Equal Justice, Grace *Britannia*'s Realm,
Records of Old may Glorious *Senates* shew,
But Greater Actions will Eternize You:
Your Country's Glory proves the *Patriots* Aim,
And latest *Annals* shall preserve your Fame.
The Publick Welfare still depends on You,
Their Hopes are Just, because their *Senate*'s True,
A *Senate* sway'd by no sinister Ends,
Their Country's Champions, and their Sov'reign's (Friends,
Whose Mutual Glory is their sole Debate,
At once to make them both Compleatly Great;
Unlike the *Poets* giddy Charioteer,
Proud of Command, press'd on with mad Career,
Mistook his Father's Road, and set the World on fire:
But as a Surgeon carefully should try,
The utmost limits of a Malady,
So when *Britannia* doth to you repair,
She hopes for none but skillful *Patriots* here.

AND

AND now behold Divine EUSEBIA stand,
A Mitre decks her Head, a Crofs her Hand;
Martyrs like Stars around her Frontlet fhine,
Her Form's as Lovely, as her Soul Divine.

And thus She Speaks.

"I Truft my fteady Champions will Difpenfe,
' With fuch a PARENT as ne'er gave Offence;
' Pleas'd as I am at *Britain*'s happy Fate,
' To fee fuch Guardians to protect her State,
' Yet give a TENDER MOTHER leave to fhare
' At leaft an equal Portion of your Care.
' Remember firft what anx'ous Care and Toil,
' I underwent to fave your groaning Ifle,
' How many Valiant Champions bravely dy'd,
' Tho' with the Rack, and fiery Tortures try'd,
' (That Man cannot be faid to die with Shame,
' Who when expiring Triumph's in his Flame.)
' Remember in my bleft ELIZA's Reign,
' When crafty *Rome* combin'd with haughty *Spain*,
' How She *Illuftrious She* Maintain'd Her Caufe,
' Sav'd my Religion, and reftor'd your Laws;

' So

'When cruel MARIE's Priests with Pleasure stood,
'Profuse of Martyrs Flames, and Sacred Blood,
'When they prophan'd the Earth with human Gore,
'And then the dismal Landskip cover'd o'er,
'With holy Ashes they had made before;
'How soon th' Almighty set *Britannia* free,
'*Remember this was done to rescue me.*
'So when the Sulph'rous Train was kindling laid
'Under that awful *Dome* in which you tread,
'The same Great Arm restrain'd the threat'ning Blow,
'*And this was done to save* EUSEBIA *too.*

'BUT when dissenting Faction highly swell'd,
'And against me, and Royal CHARLES rebell'd,
''Twas then alas! your Dear EUSEBIA bled,
'I lost my Cause, my Champion lost his Head,
'Twelve tedious Years I did my Fate deplore,
'Under the Yoke of base Usurping Pow'r,
'When a Bright Sun from long Eclipse arose,
'Gladly receiv'd by his relenting Foes,

'With welcome Rays refresh'd his Native Shore,
'And I appear'd more Glorious than before.

'WHEN JAMES by *Rome* unhappily mis-led,
'His Country's freedom, and my Rights betray'd,
'A GUARDIAN PRINCE of Eminent Renown,
'Rescu'd my Mitre, and preserv'd your Crown;
'Thus have I Triumph'd, and outbrav'd the shocks,
'Of *Popish* Shipwreck, and *Fanatick* Rocks.
'Lo, yet I see the *Hydra*'s baleful head,
'A Beast for Everlasting mischief bred,
'Her many Crowns are *Emblems* to display
'A greedy Thirst for Universal Sway,
'Her armed Heads prove Conquest is her Prey;
'But you my Faithful Champions will maintain,
'My Rights against this hideous Monster's train;
'What I have felt your Ancestors have shar'd,
'By *Senates* like your selves I've oft been spar'd,
'Thus free from fear, tho' Dangers were in view,
'I see my Welfare still confirm'd by You:

'Secure I sit and at my Altar's wait,
'Whilst in united Counsels you debate,
'How to make Glorious both your Church and State'

Of you Eusebia can no Favour ask,
But what's a *Just*, and Pleasurable task,
Her future Safety she's no cause to fear,
Whilst none but *faithful* Sons are seated here;
Astræa too revives her Golden Reign,
And *Britain*'s faded Glory blooms again,
'Tis hard for me to tell what future Joys,
Will smoothly flow from your Harmonious Voice:
Oppression is no more the poor Man's fate,
The Rich expect to be more amply Great,
The hostile Bands that envy *Britain*'s fame,
Dread such a King, and such a *Senate*'s Name;
In War there's Honour, but ten Thousand charms
In Peaceful Triumphs, more than Force of Arms,
Our Foes Compliance we may well foresee,
You always Conquer, when you all Agree;

From

From hence *Britannia* dreads no ſecret harms,
Nor fear's Succeſs if forc'd to Wars alarms,
She values not ungen'rous dark Intrigues,
Of Truſt betray'd, or violated Leagues;
The Treach'rous ſeldom Conquer, where they fight,
Succeſs attends thoſe *Patriots* who unite.

THE great Atchievements of Victorious *Rome*,
Were the Reſults of Counſels firſt at home,
Not *Scipio*'s valour can defend that Realm,
Where *Catilines* are Fav'rites at the Helm,
But laſting Glories Crown that happy ſtate,
Where SCIPIO's lead, and CICERO's debate,
Where *Senates* like your ſelves, protect their Laws,
And never Vote but for their Country's Cauſe:
Oh bleſt *Britannia*! thou whoſe Friends muſt own,
A Greater *Monarch* never fill'd thy Throne,
Nor richer Trophies grac'd thy Glorious Crown,
Trophies, which are but ſuch a PRINCE's due,
They honour Him, becauſe He honour's you.

Your faithful Actions merit Royal Love,
In such harmonious Spheres the Angels move,
Their Rev'rence flows from Nature, void of fear,
The Just return of their GREAT SOV'REIGN'S Care;
As Earthly Courts are by the same Decree,
Ordain'd for Peace and mutual Harmony,
As *Senate*'s like the sacred Choir above,
Should all unite in Loyalty and Love,
So You ILLUSTRIOUS SIRS, teach us the way,
That to be happy here, is to obey:
A Maxim ev'ry *Briton* had in view,
But never found the great *Effect* so true,
As when explain'd by Royal GEORGE and *YOU*.

FINIS.

CPSIA information can be obtained
at www.ICGtesting.com
Printed in the USA
BVHW06s1010090718
521160BV00023B/1231/P

9 781170 026144